and whispered...
Thank You

GLIAL Brain Cancer from the Caregivers Perspective

Sharon Mercer

SJ Writing Services, LLC
Publishing
Columbia, South Carolina
https://sjwritingservice9.wixsite.com/website

Scripture quotations in this book are from the New International Version (NIV) of The Holy Bible.

Editing and Book Cover Design by SJ Writing Services, LLC.

ISBN: 978-1-967699-05-6

Dedication

To my beloved husband, Chris, the strongest man -- full of courage and wisdom. He inspired each of us to keep our eyes fixed on Jesus.

To my Lord and Savior, who carries me daily and sustains me through the most challenging times.

To my family: Ryan, Becca, Daniel, and Mary Scott, who surround me with love, honor, and support.

"With a love too deep for words…"
Your Rose of Sharon
Lyrics by Mumford & Sons

Preface

In the world of oncology, no journey is ever the same, yet every journey leaves a profound impact on those who walk it. As an oncology nurse, I have had the privilege of standing beside countless patients and their loved ones through the toughest of times. However, the journey with Sharon and her husband, Chris, during their battle with glial brain cancer was particularly meaningful.

When I first met Chris, he was not just another patient; he was a man full of life, strength, and an unyielding faith. His strength and faith were mirrored by Sharon's, whose dedication and love were palpable every step of the way. From the onset, I was not just a healthcare provider but part of a team striving for something more—hope, healing, and the possibility of a miracle through experimental treatments.

In the trenches of treatment, we shared more than just the clinical aspects of care. We shared stories, fears, laughter, and tears. As the experimental treatments unfolded, so did our relationsh evolving into a bond that transcended the typical boundaries of patient and caregiver. I became an intimate part of their family, walking this journey with them. I treasured every encounter, every hug. . .Chris gave the best hugs!

This book is not just a portrayal of a medical journey, but a testament to the human spirit, to the love and dedication of a wife and a family, and to the resilience and faith found in the darkest of times. It is about the triumphs and the heartaches, the moments of hope, and the quiet acceptance that sometimes follows.

As you read this book, I hope you find a sense of understanding and connection to the complex emotions and experiences that define the caregiver's role in the battle against brain cancer. It is a role marked by profound love, immense challenges, strength, and ultimately, a deep and abiding faith and belief in God.

On a personal note:

Throughout my 30-plus years as an oncology nurse, I have often been asked how I coped with the sadness I encountered daily. My response has always been unwavering: the blessings I reaped from my relationships with my patients and their families, and the profound lessons I learned as we walked through their journeys together, touched my life in ways that made me a better person.

Michele DeCandio
RN, OCN, CCRP

Table of Contents

"*Have I not commanded you? Be
strong and courageous. Do not be
afraid; do not be discouraged, for the
LORD your God will be with you
wherever you go.*"

Joshua 1:9 (NIV)

Introduction

That's So Beautiful

Chris grew up in the church, and at the age of 34 he became a born again Christian. Every day he would diligently read and study the Bible. After memorizing a passage from the Bible he would ask the boys to follow along as he would recite verse after verse. If he missed a word, or a phrase, he would start over again until he recited it correctly. Chris had such a gift for memorizing God's Word that he had more than half of the New Testament committed to memory. There were some days I would say to Chris, "I didn't read my Bible today. Can you give me some scripture?" Immediately, he would share a verse I really needed.

It seemed odd to me that Chris had the capacity to memorize entire books of the Bible. I would ask my mom "How is it even possible for him to memorize most of the New Testament, when I have difficulty memorizing a simple paragraph?" I also would ask, "Why does he memorize so much Scripture if he is always going to have access to the Bible?" My mind couldn't understand his wonderful capability to memorize things so easily.

Fast forward to life with brain cancer. Chris found it challenging to communicate, read, write, and understand. Nevertheless, the Scripture dwelled in the deepest part of his heart and mind. When we went to church, we would sit in the back pew so that we weren't a distraction to others. We did not want anyone to be puzzled with the device on his head when he removed his baseball hat. Throughout most of the sermon, Chris would have his head bowed. He would do this so that he could listen to the pastor and not be distracted by his surroundings or other stimuli. There would be times when the pastor would read a verse from the Bible, and instantly Chris would throw up his hand and finish the rest of the verse out loud. Again, I could hardly believe it. How many times could he not remember my name - yet he could complete a Bible verse. It was truly incredible that he had God's Word hidden deep in his soul.

Chapter One

Catastrophic Shock

We rang in the New Year of 2015 with a family cruise to the Caribbean. Getting together was always enjoyable since our family is scattered across the United States. We looked forward to yummy food, lots of activities, exploring the islands, dancing the night away, and simply relaxing.

When the five days of vacation concluded we returned home to resume our normal routine. My husband Chris and I parted ways. He flew back to his new job in Lancaster, Pennsylvania while I drove back to our home in South Carolina.

After some time, my phone rang and Chris said, "*Flight not good.*"

I responded, "Flight not good? What happened?"

He kept saying, "Ummm… Uhhh … DD" as he proceeded to meet his coworker who was picking him up from the airport. He sat down. He was confused about why he couldn't remember his colleague's name. Frantically, I instructed Chris to hand the phone to someone nearby, so that I could get a better understanding of the situation. Thankfully, it was DJ. I said, "Hey! Chris can't speak right now and must be dehydrated. Sit him down and get him some water." DJ said, "Well, he can't form a sentence, and he keeps pointing to the luggage area."

Immediately after this strange phone call, I drove nine hours to Lancaster, Pennsylvania. When I arrived, I told Chris that he needed to see a doctor that night. We called our friend who was a physician and asked if he would look at Chris. John recommended that Chris see a general practitioner the following day because he suspected a transient ischemic attack (TIA). The general practitioner prescribed medicine for a headache and sent us on our way.

That night, Chris had severe headaches, causing him to be on the ground on his hands and knees. He said he felt like two-by-fours were hitting him on his head. It was so scary to watch him in pain. I had no idea what was happening. Oddly, the next day, the headache subsided.

I searched TIA on the computer, and "Dr. Google" told me that after an initial TIA, it is common to have another attack within fourteen days. So, I waited until day fifteen to drive back home to South Carolina. I wanted to return home for just a few days because we were being transferred to London, United Kingdom, for our next work assignment. After arriving back in South Carolina, I placed my phone on the charger at home and hurried off to dinner to meet our eldest son, Ryan, and my sister-in-law, Megan. During dinner, Ryan got a phone call. On the other line was DJ. He said that Chris was returning from the gym after a workout and entered his apartment off balance. Chris was speaking but could not form a complete sentence. DJ rushed him to the local emergency department where they admitted Chris. The next day, Chris' company flew me, and our youngest son, Daniel, to Pennsylvania.

The doctors ran multiple tests on Chris while he was hospitalized the following days. Despite the extensive testing, nothing was conclusive. Thankfully, Chris' company transferred us back to our hometown of Columbia, South Carolina, to be with our loved ones and have their support.

We were surrounded by Chris' family and colleagues as they checked in to see how he was doing. We were home for only four days when Chris returned to the local office for work. I finally found myself alone in our house. I was grateful for the time to pause and process the whirlwind of these recent events. I sat on the edge of the bed, looked out the window, and wondered what hospital I would take Chris to if he had another episode. I put my head in my hands and was literally visualizing how to drive to the closest hospital. *Which hospital would I go to? How would I get there?* We hadn't lived in Columbia for a year, so I really needed to get my bearings.

Then, five minutes later, my phone rang. The caller ID lit up "Lover Boy" (*i.e.* Chris' contact). Chris said, "Time tonight?"
I responded, "Time tonight for what?"
There was no response -- only silence.
I said, "Oh my gosh, Chris, it's happening again! Stay right where you are, and I'll come find you!"
I quickly grabbed my keys, got in the car without my flip-flops, and raced downtown to Chris' office. It seemed like the longest drive because of all the stoplights. Chris knew I wouldn't have the security

code to enter his office building, so he waited outside on the street corner.

While driving, I contacted Chris's colleague, Sunil, to explain what was happening. Sunil went looking for Chris and explained the situation to their CEO. They found him outside and urged him to get into the car. Chris was visibly confused and upset and wanted to wait for me. I spoke with Chris on his colleague's cellphone and instructed him with the following words…"They are taking you to the hospital. I'll meet you there! Get in their car!"

This episode lasted several hours, with Chris unable to comprehend or speak. At 2 A.M., the neurologist came into our room and told us that Chris had a primary brain tumor.

When the neurologist left the room, Chris was still foggy and very tired from the episode. Despite the delirium, my husband confidently said, "The Lord gave and the Lord has taken away. Blessed be the name of the Lord." (Job 1:21b; NASB). After saying these words, he peacefully fell asleep.

I was in shock to hear the doctor's findings. I sadly just knelt on the cold hospital floor at Chris' feet and prayed throughout the night. Our extended family arrived early in the morning to comfort us.

They were present with us when the neurology team explained the results from the brain MRI.

After he had a brain biopsy performed on the lesion, the doctor walked into the room. Typically, the attending physician would have several residents and fellows following him into the room as they consulted patients. However, this time, he entered alone. The look on his face said it all. He shared the impression by showing us a sheet of paper -- "Primary malignancy glial brain tumor; grade 3 or 4."

He sternly and clearly instructed us to go to Duke due to the complexity and severity of the diagnosis. Our hearts sank, but we heeded his advice and traveled to Duke four days later. It was at this point, I realized we had embarked on a long, life-altering medical journey that would change our lives forever.

Sharon, Ryan, and Chris

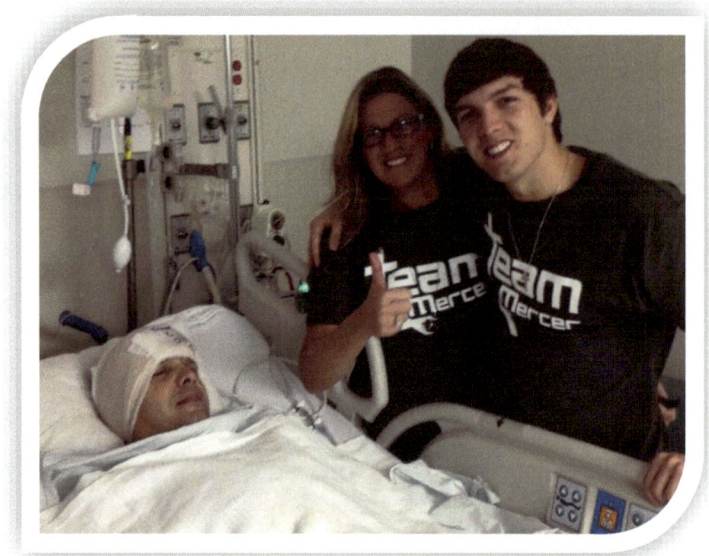

(Chris's Family)
Rich, Ellen, Mary, EJ, Judy, Chris, Carol, and Ed

Chris, Carol, and Rich

Sandy McGukin, Arindrita, baby,
Lingaraj, Chris, Sunil, Sharon, Jenni

Carol (Chris's Mom) and Chris

"Come to me, all you who are weary and burdened, and I will give you rest. Take my yoke upon you, and learn from me, for I am gentle and humble in heart, and you will find rest for your souls. For my yoke is easy and my burden is light."

Matthew 11:28-30 (NIV)

Chapter Two

Selah

Living in Lancaster, Pennsylvania before Chris received his diagnosis was like having a second honeymoon. It was a gift of God's sweet pause before the storm. God gave us the Miller family – who were our best friends in Pennsylvania and remain our best friends to this day. We were empty nesters with a better work-life balance and with more time to sightsee. We lived near the Amish community and spent our time exploring many small, neighborly towns. Our weekends were filled with adventures. For fun, we would purposefully try to get lost on a random country backroad. Then we would turn our GPS on to find our way back home. We loved it all – the slow living, the covered bridges, the Amish families driving their horse and buggy, the incredible sunsets over the Susquehanna River, and the glorious farmland.

On other weekends, we would leave our home to travel to Baltimore, Philadelphia, or Cape

May for the weekend. I was extremely grateful for the quality time these getaways provided for me to make memories with my husband. Pennsylvania was truly a charming place to live, and it was a beautiful time in our marriage.

However, not everything was perfect. While we were in Pennsylvania, sometimes things seemed off with Chris. Looking back, there were several things I can recall that made me feel like I was walking on eggshells so that I wouldn't disappoint Chris. One evening, we were attending a company dinner. When we exited the car, he asked for his cell phone. I went to pass him the phone, and we fumbled the phone. It dropped on the ground and shattered. Unfortunately, this happened on three separate occasions. Needless to say, I quickly became friends with the local phone repair man at the mall.

Next, another odd thing happened. One day, when we were having lunch at our tiny apartment, I made Chris some lunch and placed his drink on the table. I went to the kitchen, which was twenty steps away, but when I came back, his drink had fallen on the floor. Chris was frustrated at me and said, "Why did you put the drink on the edge of the table?" Of course, I was apologetic because I had no idea how I could be so careless.

In hindsight, there were several other instances like these. For example, one time we were leaving the parking lot of a grocery store, and Chris was driving. He kept hesitating. He couldn't determine whether to turn right or left at the stop sign. He would start to drive, then stop, back up, and then start driving slowly again towards the stop sign. It was definitely odd. We got home from the store with groceries in hand, and Chris was going up the stairs to our third-floor apartment. He was taking the stairs two at a time, lost his balance, and fell. He hurried into the apartment and didn't say a word. He just threw the groceries on the counter, laid down on the couch, and slept for several hours. This was by no means a normal happening for him.

One other story I remember is when Chris was speaking on the phone with his CEO. He was speaking loudly and boldly on the phone. When he had hung up the phone, I said, "Chris, I don't know if you realize it, but you sounded really boastful on that call."

When Chris received his brain cancer diagnosis in February 2015, I realized the things I had witnessed during the previous year were the reason for the oddities. These stories confirmed that Chris was having issues with personality change, mental processing, vision, and balance due to his tumor even before he was diagnosed.

Sandy & Dave Miller, Sharon, and Chris

"My flesh and my heart may fail, but God is the strength of my heart and my portion forever."

Psalm 73:26 (NIV)

Chapter Three

Gospel, Glory, Growth

For most of his adult life, Chris wanted nothing more than to share Christ with others. In tough times he was even more adamant about spreading the good news about God. He focused on what he called, "The 3G's" (*ie.* Gospel, Glory, and Growth). Even through the trials, Chris recognized God's sovereignty, and wanted his health journey to be used to:

- Spread the Gospel
- Recognize God's glory
- Grow himself and others closer to God

Chris wanted God's character in his life to be shown despite his cancer diagnosis. My husband told me, "I will continue to walk this journey with Jesus. I would much rather walk this path with Him, than walk a primrose path without Him." This verse sums it up best -- "For to me, to live is Christ and to die is gain" Philippians 1:21 (NIV).

On February 28, 2015, Chris had a craniotomy performed at Duke. Those who loved him most were praying nearby in the waiting room. His surgery was successful. He recovered at a hotel near the hospital until his follow-up visit the following week. Richard, Chris' twin brother, was quite the teammate in Chris' recovery. On the fourth day of recovery, Chris woke up crying, "Jesus, Jesus." He said, "Sharon, all I had was the name of Jesus, and I didn't even know if I had that correct." The swelling from the surgery had caused edema and he was unable to speak or to think until this specific morning. I was so glad to hear his voice again, and from this moment forward, I anticipated his health would be restored.

His final pathology report came back as 'anaplastic astrocytoma grade III', which is a high-grade, aggressive glioma. Chris did not want to know his diagnosis, so I carried the knowledge of this horrific diagnosis all alone. It was a heavy burden to carry by myself. Later on, he acknowledged the heaviness I carried for both of us.

Chris was placed on standard of care (SOC) treatment for his glioma for the first ten months.

Despite this treatment, the tumor progressed to involve a separate area of his brain. At this point, the tumor was deemed inoperable and we truly appreciated the seriousness of the disease.

My sister-in-law, Judy, is a "Rockstar". Her nature is to always be available. We must have put her nature to the test because we needed her help many times and in many ways. This was a long journey with constant ups and downs. Judy would often relieve me of my duties when we had to go to the emergency department for Chris' seizures. She said, "Chris has an entire neurology team tending to him. I'm here to check on you and see how I can help." Then she would hand me a piece of dark chocolate to convey the message, "I'm here, and we got this." It was just the support I needed to be reassured that I was never alone.

Since SOC therapy failed, our only option was to find a research trial that Chris would qualify for. We worked tirelessly for a week searching out options. When it was all said and done, we found 152 trials of interest. We organized them into piles based on inclusion and exclusion criteria. Judy helped me parse through each trial, which helped me narrow it down to two options. Out of the 152 trials being conducted, he was only a candidate for two of them. God provided two options, but we only needed one. After weighing our two options, we settled on the Tocagen clinical trial. Thankfully, there was an opening for seven applicants at the Medical University of South Carolina (MUSC), which was located nearby. The trial had a treatment group and control group. The treatment group would receive the Toca-511 virus, while the control group would be treated with SOC.

In order to have Chris considered for enrollment in the study, we had to deliver the MRI disc to MUSC for review. I called our son Ryan, who was enrolled as a medical student at MUSC during this time. To our surprise, when he answered the phone, he informed us that he was on rotation with the neuro-oncologist that would eventually be Chris' doctor. When Ryan arrived at the car, I handed him the disc, and we hopped right back on the highway to go home and wait patiently for a phone call.

When we finally received the phone call, we were relieved to find out Chris would be enrolled in the Tocagen trial. After completing the necessary consent forms, the plan was to have surgery performed to inject the Toca-511 virus directly into the tumor. The surgery went well, but after surgery he couldn't stop vomiting. It was awful, and I knew this wasn't normal because it didn't happen with the previous surgery at Duke. When the surgeon made his morning rounds, he heard my concern, and they performed an emergency craniotomy for a perioperative brain bleed. Chris now had a deficit in his visual field to the right of midline. The neurosurgeon encouraged me to stay on his right side so Chris would track my voice to the right and search for me. Essentially, half his world was invisible. At first, he would bump into things, but with time he became more aware of his surroundings. I was honored to hold Chris' right hand as he learned to navigate his new environment.

Immediately after the second craniotomy was performed to resolve his brain bleed, Chris didn't know his name and couldn't identify common objects. It was extremely scary.

Listening to music was the only thing that soothed him. In order to put him at ease, he would play the same song over and over. The song was written by STEPL, which was a quartet that worships at our church and sings during our Christmas programs. They performed a song called "I Can See the Light", and Chris loved listening to it. He found perfect peace and comfort whenever he heard the song. Often, I would see him remove his glasses to wipe away a tear. If someone walked into his hospital room, he would pause the song. He waited until they finished their work, left the room, and then he would start the song from the very beginning. He had it on repeat… 24/7.

After Chris healed from his surgeries, the Tocagen trial required him to take thirteen pills three times a day. In addition, he had to take anti-epileptics and anti-depressants. In total, he would have to take fifty-three pills every day during his clinic week. The trial would require him to take numerous medications, attend countless consults, and undergo several MRI scans over the course of two years. Our lives and schedules had once again changed.

We set alarms throughout the day to remind Chris to take his medication. We prepared meals for Chris to eat in the middle of the night when he had to take his nighttime dose of medication. We embraced life the best we could. We adapted our lives the best we knew how to allow Chris to experience life as normal as possible.

Charleston, South Carolina is ranked the No. 1 small historic city in America, and it quickly became our second home as we visited the doctor at MUSC on a regular basis. We utilized the MUSC medical patient rate at the Marriott Courtyard Charleston Waterfront. The staff quickly became family to us. They were always interested in how Chris was doing after his consultation with the doctor. Deborah, the breakfast host, would ensure Chris had breakfast ordered to his liking. Chris was treated like royalty at the Marriott. They welcomed us as family and encouraged us throughout our journey.

Judy, Sharon, Chris, and Carol

Deborah and Sharon

Chapter Four

Genius Amplifier

The Duke and MUSC neurology teams strongly encouraged us to hold on to hope. If one therapy wasn't working, there would be other options to try in the future. Unfortunately, Chris' tumor progressed despite being on the Tocagen trial. Because of this, Chris began therapy with bevacizumab infusions every two weeks, as well as, Optune Tumor Treating Field (TTF). Meanwhile he would continue Tocagen.

Optune therapy is a wearable, portable TTF device that affects tumor cell division to prevent tumor growth. It was overwhelming when I was first trained on how to use the Optune device. In the beginning, I spent forty minutes changing the arrays to position them effectively. However, just a few weeks later, Chris and I had a system in place where we could complete the process in only five minutes. We trained a few other family members on how to position the Optune device just in case I was not available.

Since we live in the south where it is hot and humid, we had to replace the Optune arrays every one or two days. The arrays consisted of 36 electrodes applied to the scalp with adhesive. The cords and portable battery pack weighed eight pounds. For fun, we would use a permanent marker to write Scripture on the electrode patches. On other occasions, we would write gameday quotes like … 'Go Gamecocks!' It was entertaining to watch Chris remove the hat he wore over the electrode pads and transform into a walking billboard.

It took us several days to grow accustomed to any new treatment, but we would quickly find our 'new normal'. Optune was no different and sometimes we had to find ways to adapt. For example, when we were at the beach, Chris was able to join us near the ocean despite being surrounded by sand and water. To make it all work, we would place the battery pack in a clean garbage bag so the device didn't get sandy or wet. To make him more comfortable, we purchased a hat with an attached solar-powered fan. This fancy fan kept his electrodes from overheating. As a finishing touch, we set up a chair under a beach umbrella to provide him with adequate shade. It took a little planning and effort, but it was doable. My brother, Larry, used to call his Optune device 'The Genius Amplifier'. Larry would say Chris was smarter than him despite having brain cancer.

Chris and Sharon
~ How we do life ~

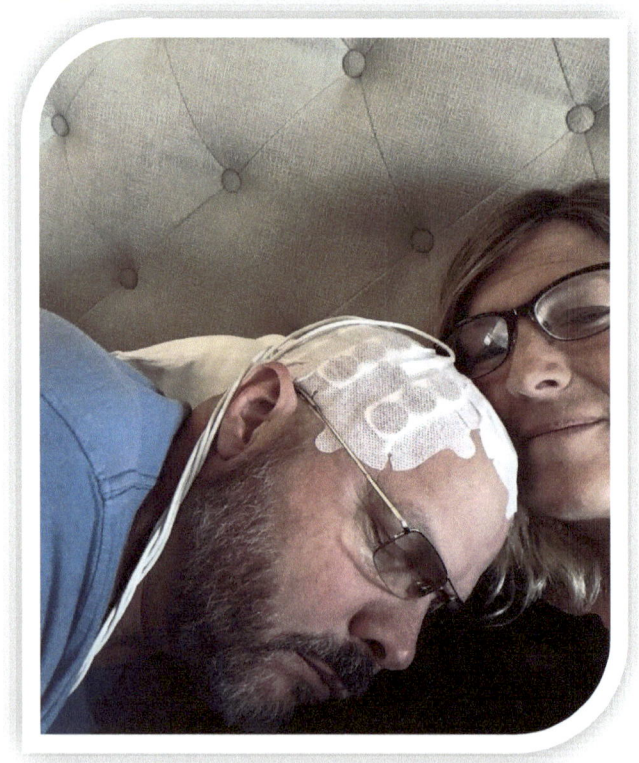

Chris and Sharon with 1ˢᵗ grandbaby, Hampton

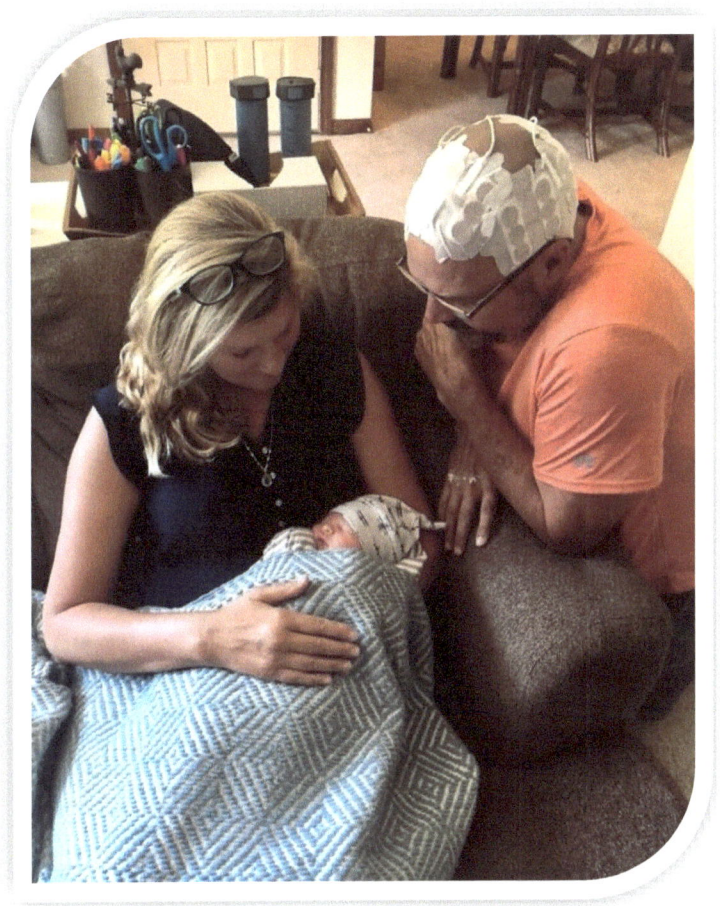

"When you pass through the waters, I will be with you; and when you pass through the rivers, they will not sweep over you. When thou walk through the fire, you will not be burned; the flames will not set you ablaze."

Isaiah 43:2 (NIV)

Chapter Five

Girlfriend

I took an overnight respite at a Bed & Breakfast and was looking forward to getting a few minutes to relax by myself. I was so physically and emotionally tired in every way. I only brought some clothes, my Bible, and some books. The first morning, my quiet time was in Paul's second letter to the Corinthians. The verse said, "Who comforts us in all our troubles, so that we can comfort those in any trouble with the comfort we ourselves receive from God" (2 Corinthians 1:4, NIV). Boom! I closed my Bible and said to myself, "Wow, maybe what has caused us so much pain would become a place of purpose." Reading this verse, caused me to ponder what God was preparing for us in the midst of this difficult time.

These events occurred in June 2018. A month later, our medical team suggested that we remain in the waiting room following the consult. The doctor suggested that someone may want to speak with us about our journey. We remained in the waiting room for several hours before a couple walked by and noticed Chris wearing the Optune device. They stopped and inquired about it. We shared Chris' brain cancer story, and then listened to their own brain cancer story. We soon began to walk alongside them. Our families cared for each other, checked in on each other, and arranged time to meet together after clinic visits.

The highlight of our clinic days was seeing Chris' friends, doctors, and caregivers that God placed on our path. We developed several meaningful relationships because of Chris' brain cancer diagnosis. I recall one day at MUSC particularly well. We had already met with the neuro-oncology team, and they asked us to remain in the consult room. The nurse shared that there was a 22-year-old female recently diagnosed, and her tumor was deemed inoperable because of its location. My heart dropped, and I prayed silently with my head in my hands. They entered the room, and we met a beautiful young lady with brain cancer named Kyla. We also met Jo (*ie.* her mother), as well as, several other family members.

We visited briefly and then exchanged contact numbers to remain in touch.

Initially, I would text Kyla to say 'Hi' and we would compare notes to see how she and Chris were doing with treatment. Oftentimes, we would reschedule our appointments to make Chris' appointment overlap with her appointment. It was imperative that I see her smiling face and give her a hug. Likewise, I also knew how important it was for Kyla and Chris to be together because they shared a special friendship. I took a photo of Kyla and Chris from the 'Head for the Cure (HFTC) Fundraiser Walk/Run' to tape to our kitchen door. Every time I exited our kitchen, I would see the photo, say a prayer, kiss my hand, and tap the picture. Truly, it was a way of me saying, "God, please meet all of their needs for this day!"

In one instance, Chris was thinking about Kyla but couldn't recall her name. As a result, he would say, "I wonder how she is doing?"
I would respond, "Who are you talking about?"
"Girlfriend," he said.
So, from that point on, 'girlfriend' was our code name for Kyla.

As time passed, I was unable to communicate with Kyla, so I started reaching out to her mom through text. Kyla passed at the young age of 25 and left a courageous legacy behind. She had a constant and contagious smile. She was beautiful, brilliant, full of joy and laughter, and extraordinarily strong in adversity. Now, her mom carries Kyla's torch, fundraising for HFTC Foundation (#TeamKyla) and advocating for the National Brain Tumor Society community. Jo and I have sadly walked similar journeys. We have loved and cared for each other through the most difficult times, and we are locked 'arm-in-arm' forever because of it. I am full of gratitude to our neuro-oncology staff for introducing us to each other because it has been an amazing blessing.

Despite brain cancer being a devastating diagnosis, it has allowed us to create wonderful lifelong relationships with beautiful families like Kyla's.

Chris and Kyla (Girlfriend)

Chris and Kyla (Girlfriend)

Sharon and Jo (Kyla's Mom)

Chapter Six

God's Tapestry

Chris underwent Stereotactic Radiation Therapy because of more medical issues. He was recovering well, yet after several weeks, he was still down and depressed. I was familiar with his mood changes, but I was not familiar with how gloomy he was becoming.

One afternoon, I sat down on the couch beside him, and he shared that he couldn't understand why he was still alive when everyone else was passing – a form of survivor's guilt. His quality of life and abilities were limited to picking up pinecones and walking the dog around the block. I reassured him that he had so much purpose, that I needed him, and that his family needed him. Additionally, I shared with him what a powerful witness he was to others by always being content and remaining focused on their needs. Plus, he offered the biggest smile to everyone that he met!

We talked about grief. I explained that I also share grief as a caregiver -- anticipatory grief. I held his hand and gently said to him, "Chris, I can't control your diagnosis, and I can't cure your diagnosis. However, what I do know is that I am called to love and cherish you and trust God at every moment. It's the only way, and even with the complexities of this disease, it has to be enough. Because God is always going to be our *enough*."

Then I reminded Chris we have so much! I said, "Remember, 'Gospel, Glory, Growth.' You always say God makes up the margin for what we need." So, as we sat on the couch that day, I prayed for Chris. I prayed specifically that God would use him and that he would see that God had a purpose for him even during these challenging days.

One of the issues with Chris' brain tumor was that he would ruminate. He would have something on his mind and talk about it continually throughout the day. He just couldn't let it go. I always tried to help him get his checklist complete, so that his mind could rest. This would provide me with a much-needed break! However, it was like playing chess because somehow, he was always one step ahead. Let's just say that his checklist was never complete and I never reached the window of rest I needed, which was at times exhausting!

One morning, I had a few minutes of uninterrupted time while drinking my coffee. I thought to myself, "I'm going to get rid of this security alarm panel that is driving Chris crazy."
So, I called the security company and said, "Hello, this is Sharon and Chris Mercer. We no longer use our alarm system and would like the panel and the sensors to be removed." The lady responded, "I'm sorry your contract is finished, and you own it. We can't do anything for you."

So, I called another home security company and said, "Hello! This is Sharon Mercer. We were wondering if you could send a representative to get our alarm panel off the wall, windows, and doors." She said, "Oh, dear. I can email you a YouTube video to learn how to disengage it and remove everything yourself." I hung up the phone and thought, "Umm, girl, you have no idea about my life. I cannot do one more thing -- ugh!!!"

So, I called a third home security company and used the 'cancer card' this time. We pretty much used the 'cancer card' once a day. I said, "Hey, this is Sharon Mercer. We have an alarm panel that needs to come down, and I need to have it come down because my husband has brain cancer, and it's irritating him."

They replied, "I will send someone right over."

Within one hour, the technician was knocking on my kitchen door. I welcomed him in and said, "Hi, my husband has brain cancer. He has aphasia, and he just had a big treatment. Please be patient with him. He will want to talk to you about every sensor on every window and on every door. It will take him some time to process his words, so please be very patient."

I woke Chris up, and he came out of the bedroom without wearing his baseball hat. The technician said, "Is that Optune?"

I turned around to look at him with the biggest surprised eyes! I asked, "How do you know about Optune?"

He said, "I was diagnosed with glioblastoma (GBM) and the doctors will start me on Optune this week."

Oh my goodness! Only God could have brought him to our kitchen door. It probably took the representative only fifteen minutes to remove the alarm equipment. He stayed and visited for three hours. It was now very clear to Chris that God was still using him to encourage and support those with this difficult disease. This indeed was his purpose. At the time, Optune was used by only 10,000 GBM patients worldwide. His name was Kyle. He was 29 years old when we met him. We had Kyle at our house every month for lunch, and Chris shared Christ with him and was the truest inspiration. Sadly, Kyle passed away several months later.

"It was never about the alarm system
And it never is…it was all about
THE TAPESTRY OF GOD."

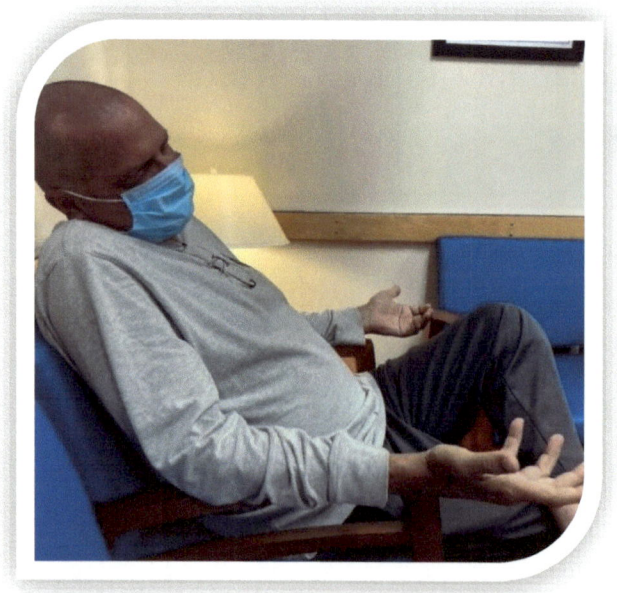

Chapter Seven

Gracious Day!

Chris kept me on my toes. Every day was different and every day was interesting. One morning, he woke me up by repeating these words, "Five times hurt!"

I responded, "Five times hurt? What is hurting you?"

He couldn't gather his words enough to make a sentence, so I quickly rose from my bed and followed him into the kitchen. He proceeded to show me that he was using 'All-Purpose cleaner' and a toothpick to remove gunk from the grooves of our electrical socket.

I thought to myself, "Oh, my word!"

All this time, he was getting shocked while playing with the electrical outlet and wearing his Optune. My heart sank, and I felt awful for him. This was just one of many stories that shed a glimmer of light on our situation.

Another example of how interesting life became involved one of Chris' newfound passions. Chris loved to do yard work. Part of his routine was to use our leaf blower to clear off the driveway three times a day. On one occasion, I heard the leaf blower being used … in the house. So, I set off to investigate the situation. He was using lawn equipment to rid the kitchen cabinets and drawers of every crumb. It was an almost brilliant idea.

Another time, I heard our dog Millie barking frantically. I turned to Chris and asked him, "Oh my gosh, what is going on with her?"
He said, "She stunk, so I sprayed her!"
I was concerned and responded, "What are you spraying her with?" With no response, I followed him to the kitchen. Chris picked up the household cleaner he used to spray her. It was Furniture polish. Oh, my goodness!

One morning, I was showering, and Chris came to me very upset. He started yelling, "This guy cussed me out!"
I responded, "What do you mean? Who cussed you out?"

He said, "This guy… the neighbor… he cussed me out."

I said, "Oh my gosh, what are you even talking about?"

He responded with, "And … I drove," and handed me the keys.

I said, "Oh my word Chris, you can't drive the car." We hopped in the car and he directed me from the passenger seat where to go. We drove down the road and pulled up by a tree near a stop sign. The neighbor was still out on the patio. I exclaimed, "Hey, did you cuss my husband out?"

He responded, "Yeah, I did, because I had no idea what he was getting out of the trunk of his car. He got a garbage tarp of stuff out of the trunk and pushed it down my storm drain. Then he reached out his hand to introduce himself to me and he couldn't say his name and had these tracks on his arms and legs. I thought he was crazy."

I said, "No that's not it at all. He has brain cancer and can't find his words." I knew exactly what Chris was wanting to accomplish. Chris wanted to get the debris from our yard and get rid of it instead of waiting until the yard-waste pickup day. It was difficult for Chris to navigate his life at times.

During the journey, I wanted to be more for him… always more.

Working the television remote was challenging for Chris. Electronics, sadly, were no longer his friend. We had a small television on the back patio where he enjoyed watching the classic black and white television shows. His favorite shows were Bonanza, Andy Griffith, and Perry Mason. One evening, Chris couldn't get the television to turn on, so I tried to fix it, but to no avail. The following morning, he was working on 'a project' in the basement. It always made me happy when Chris was working on a project because I knew he was being productive and it made him feel like he had purpose. That is, until he showed me the 16 feet of cable he had cut. Then he said, "Will you please call the cable company to come fix this mess?" Needless to say, the cable company technicians were frequent visitors to our house during this season. In fact, one technician gave me his personal cell phone number as a direct line because of the frequent issues we had with our cable.

Another time something really strange happened. Chris was going to make his lunch and yelled out, "Where's the bread?" I stopped whatever I was doing at the time and went to the kitchen. I checked everywhere for the bread but couldn't find it. It didn't really bother me, because I knew we would find it at some point. After all, one time I found the ketchup bottle in the laundry basket. Regardless, I made a different lunch for him and thought to myself, "No big deal, I can go by the grocery store later today and grab us some bread." One of my helpful strategies was to assist Chris by redirecting him. This way he wasn't consumed by something or easily frustrated. About an hour later, Chris said, "Somebody broke into our house and stole our bread, and now they are looking for drugs."

I said, "Chris, why do you say that?"

He said, "Come look." He guided me to the hallway where our linen cabinet was located. He showed me a screw that had fallen from the hinge door and was lying on the floor. The cabinet door was hanging at an angle.

I explained to him that we only have towels, Band-Aids, and cotton balls in the hallway closet. All the chemotherapy drugs were in a separate location. For the next two hours, he urged me to call the police and inform them that someone had committed theft – in his mind, someone had stolen our bread and drugs. Gracious Day! Another long day and it made my stomach curl because of his psychosis. There were some hard days. I found that it was important to remain rational, speak gently to him, and listen to him so that he felt heard. Despite this approach, it remained difficult to understand the message he was trying to convey to me.

Early one morning, Chris had a seizure, which I initially tried to handle from home. Chris' condition was declining quickly and I wanted to get him to MUSC as soon as possible. I knew that his oncologist would want Chris in the same MRI machine since he was on the government clinical trial. We were about 45 minutes outside of Charleston when Chris started vomiting uncontrollably. Without warning, he flung his passenger door open while we were driving on the interstate at 65 mph. I quickly glanced over my shoulder and merged lanes to pull onto the shoulder of the road.

I kept telling him, "Close the door, close the door, just throw up in the car. It's okay!" He kept slamming the door, but it wouldn't shut. I got out of the car and cautiously walked to the other side.

The latch got stuck and the door wouldn't shut for him. Thankfully, I was able to fix the door and explained to him that he cannot open the door while we are driving down the interstate. It was an enormous amount of energy to understand the simplest of things. I kept telling myself, "I am fine. We are going to be fine." Reciting these words to myself was my personal coping mechanism to protect, convince, and support us through these stressful moments. It was a lot to emotionally handle.

Chris' favorite activity was to go to a hardware store and look around. We visited Ace Hardware, Lowe's, or Harbor Freight at least fifteen times a month. Chris loved to walk up and down each aisle. One day he was determined to purchase a new patio light. He was particularly interested in purchasing a new modern light fixture, even though the light fixture we owned worked perfectly well. When we got home, Chris opened the box, and the light fixture dropped and shattered. Glass shards were everywhere, and I knew that Chris was starting to get agitated. I paused, took a deep breath, and exhaled slowly. I said to him, "Oh

Chris, not to worry. Please go back inside and I can take care of it."

I didn't want him to get any glass on his feet since he was only wearing sandals. I started cleaning up the glass with the Shop-Vac, when Chris opened the door and stated, "I'm going for a walk!"

I said calmly, "Okay, honey."

It was about 8:15 PM. He would normally walk the dog around the block every day for about 20 minutes. That was his routine when he went on a walk. Before long, it was 9:15 PM. I wondered where he was, so I called his phone, and it was turned off. We have the Life360 app, which allows for location notifications when tracking your family members. I got in the car and drove around the block but couldn't find him. It was completely dark. I was starting to get worried, so I called the police. The police officer showed up and started asking me rapid-fire questions about Chris. I'm telling him, "My husband has brain cancer. He was wearing sweatpants and a gray long-sleeve shirt."

The police officer says, "What color hair does he have?"

I responded, "He doesn't have hair. He wears these white patches and wires on his head and carries a satchel bag on the side of his body."

The last location his cell phone picked up was at the spillway between two lakes in our area – Arcadia Lakes and Forest Lake.

I asked a neighbor to stay at the house so they could call me if Chris returned. I drove my car to the spillway between the two lakes, and the police officer followed me with three other patrol cars arriving soon after. They were saying something about the lake, so I interjected and said, "My husband was the University swim team captain. He can swim well. He's not here."

Four hours later at 11:15 PM, Chris' phone comes back on, and it pings his updated location at Palmetto Assisted Living. The officers went to the location while I followed behind in my car. I told the police, "When you find him, please keep him there."

They found him sitting on a bench outside the facility. The policeman told Chris, "We have to stay here. There's a lot of people out looking for you." When I got there, my stomach was in knots, and my body was literally shaking. When I saw him, I said, "Chris, I was so worried about you. I had no idea what had happened. Why didn't you call me? Why did you turn your phone off?"

He said, "I wanted to be as close as possible to Grandma Wiegand. She's the only one who understands me. I turned my phone off because I knew I could turn it on and find my way home if I got lost."

He had limited vision, yet he had walked four miles in the dark through an area of town most would avoid at night. I don't know how he got there. It was probably not the straightest path. I was still shaking when we returned to our house, and Chris said he was tired and wanted to go to bed.

I said, "Oh my gosh, Chris we cannot go to bed. We need to talk about this!"

Chris said, "Sharon, this is just like if you went to the grocery store, and you didn't bring your phone."

I stated, "No, honey… It's not." But then, I just dropped the whole conversation because I knew he couldn't understand, and he was utterly despondent.

The next morning, while we were having coffee, I approached the day with a slow pace. I spoke softly and gently to him. I asked him, "What made you want to go to Palmetto Assisted Living?"

He said, "Because I am so frustrated and I can't do the simplest of things. I can't think easily. Everything is so hard, and nobody has any idea how hard things are for me. Your mom understood because she also had a problem with thinking."

He was referring to my mother who had dementia and recently passed away just two weeks prior from Parkinson's disease. After talking to the brain tumor counselors and sharing about our eventful evening, they suggested I find a grief counselor to help Chris process my mom's passing. Needless to say, it was a tough night. Navigating brain cancer and the associated behavioral side effects proved difficult. We relied on God to strengthen and equip us every day, and we learned to pivot along the way.

"For to me, to live is Christ

And to die is gain."

Philippians 1:21(NIV)

Chapter Eight

In Awe

I developed rheumatoid arthritis (RA) several months after Chris was diagnosed with brain cancer. Initially, I tried to treat my RA by adhering to a strict dietary regimen but eventually was started on prescription medication to help alleviate my symptoms. One day, during Chris' MUSC clinic, I went into Chris' consult with crutches because of a bad flare. Chris' neuro-oncologist said, "I know of an excellent RA doctor if you need a recommendation."

Later, for insurance reasons, I was ready to seek a referral to another RA specialist. Therefore, I reached out to Chris' neuro-oncologist via his online patient portal and wrote, "I'm ready for your RA referral." He messaged back with three doctors' names. I googled each one and settled upon the pretty blonde lady doctor.

I went to my first RA consult with my new doctor, shared with her my health history, and then my phone rang. It was Ryan, our oldest son. I whispered, "Ryan, I can't talk right now because I'm in a consult."

I quickly hung up on him and said, "I am so sorry. Of all people, I should know to have my phone off during consults."

She replied, "Oh, that's okay, that happens to my husband all the time,"

I said, "Oh, who is your husband? Is he a doctor"

She answered, "My husband is a neuro-oncologist."

Chris and I looked at each other in shock. We proceeded to share with her that we were the Mercer's who sent you the stuffed bunnies when your babies were born. We were the Mercer's who send your family our Christmas card every year.

She laughed and said, "I know who you are!" It was quite the realization. We couldn't believe that somehow God thought that Chris and I needed a doctor 'team' to navigate our health journeys. We are forever thankful for this power couple who loved and cared for us.

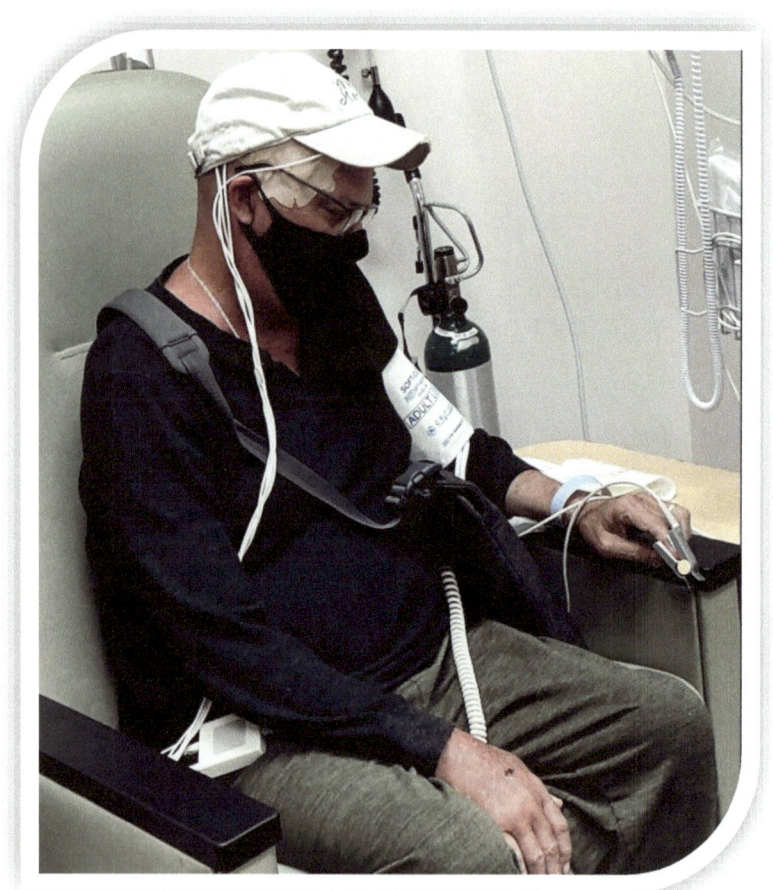

Chapter Nine

It Takes A Village

Chris' diagnosis made me feel like I was riding a rollercoaster of emotions. I often cried at night when my body finally slowed down and my mind could process the entire day. It was at these times of sheer exhaustion and anxiety when I would think to myself how I was trying to survive whatever the next day would bring. When I recognized this, I was really scared. I knew I was in a bad place and needed help. First and foremost, I needed help from God. Next, we needed help from the brain cancer organizations who sympathized and advocated for us.

These words from the Bible were fixed in my heart and mind:
"In my distress, I called to the Lord; I cried to my God for help. From his temple, he heard my voice; my cry came before him, into his ears." Psalm 18:6

Next, I would tap into my social worker resources and patient services. My first call was always to Vince Rock. Vince oversees the Care Line at American Brain Tumor Association (ABTA), which is dedicated to supporting patients and caregivers. He is an incredible listener and understands the emotional and psychological impacts of brain cancer. He consistently inquired about Chris and his current treatment program. He would patiently listen to me to determine how he could offer the best support. It was easy to share my concerns and hardships with Vince since he had heard hundreds of similar stories from other families dealing with the same hardships as us.

Throughout the years, Vince was a steady and valuable resource. He provided a list of support groups, provided access to various housing and gas reimbursement programs, and suggested organizations that would assist with financial support.

ABTA was particularly helpful in pairing me with a mentor, Robin Mahon, who had walked through a similar journey just a few years prior. I will never forget how ABTA was able to pair me with such a wonderful person like her to get me through the toughest times.

I went on to contact the Brain Tumor Network organization. The senior oncology nurse navigator, Kelly Glover, became an essential part of our care team. Kelly had a heart of empathy and understood our daily obstacles. She was a great cheerleader because she would rejoice with any triumphs that came our way.

Each call with Kelly began by providing her with updates about Chris. We would update her about Chris' current treatment and overall well-being. Next, she would take the initiative to check in on me because she understood the stressors and strains placed on a caregiver. As a nurse navigator, Kelly was able to explain Chris's lab reports, test results, and clinical treatments in a way I could understand. I would leave our conversations more empowered and focused on how to help Chris best. Kelly was indeed a safe place, as well as, a source of strength and comfort during those tough times.

These brain tumor organizations were pivotal in helping me navigate Chris' disease. I am grateful for their dedication, devotion, and passion for helping brain cancer families.

Chapter Ten

Hooray For Today!

"This is the day that the LORD has made; let us rejoice and be glad in it." *Psalm 118:24* (ESV).

My sister-in-law, Ellen, would periodically call and tell me, "Hooray for today!"

She said, "Sharon, every day when I open my eyes, I thank the Lord for the gift that this day represents."

I loved and needed this gentle reminder, yet everything hurt in my innermost being. We had a crushing diagnosis, constant unknowns, demanding treatments, and new challenges that awaited us every day. Despite these truths, I wanted to be present and cling to each day with a heart of thanksgiving. With God's strength, I aimed to help Chris live abundantly no matter how that day might look.

Chris and I would often make plans and then have to cancel them due to how he was feeling. However, people were very understanding and full of grace. We found making plans at the last minute seemed easier.

Cultivating life with Chris looked different each day. For example, one morning we were enjoying our coffee in the family room before church. I went to take my shower and get ready. Fifteen minutes later, I came into the room and saw Chris bending over, trying to tie his shoes. His hands were about two inches away from his shoes. I went over to help him and put his hand on the shoelaces. I noticed he could not even grab the laces. Immediately, I realized he had a seizure, so I started performing a basic neurological evaluation in our family room. Because Chris' tumor was on the left side of his brain, his right side would become partially paralyzed when he had a seizure. I checked for numbness on each side of his body, and assessed if he could understand simple commands. If he failed my basic neurological assessment, then we would rush to the emergency department because I knew he would be experiencing debilitating headaches and nausea in a matter of minutes. Our entire day changed in fifteen minutes. Sadly, this was quite normal. When you start to know the security guards at the hospital, then you are probably going to the hospital more than you would like.

Another difficulty came about when we would reminisce about the moments of the day. Unfortunately, Chris could not remember anything about his day. He would say, "I don't think I did anything today." Trying to help jog his memory, I would say, "Oh, do you remember you walked the dog today? You also worked in the yard. Then, we visited your mom on the way to your doctor's appointment." He enjoyed hearing about his day, and I always wanted him to understand how full, productive, and meaningful his day was. This is how our nightly dinner conversation would end before he would settle in for the evening.

At the conclusion of every evening, I would evaluate our day. I pondered how to help him better the next day. I'd ask questions such as:

- "What could I have done differently to assist him in this situation, or in that situation?"
- "How could I be more patient with his mood swings?"
- "How could I adjust his surroundings to make life easier for him?"

Then, I would start planning the logistics for the next day. Time management was crucial because of his numerous appointments that consumed a significant portion of our day. Despite the time crunches, we always found a way to add some nuggets of fun into our day.

Every day was different, but there were pockets of joy. On those 'off' days, we would stay home and lay in bed next to each other. He would sleep, and I would listen to my music. It was simple, but priceless. At least we were together.

Even when we found ourselves in the emergency department, I would sit in a plastic chair beside him and try to snuggle with him as we shared his pillow. Whether it was a spontaneous lunch date, sitting on a park swing together, or taking a short leisurely walk, we always tried to savor and embrace the small, sweet moments. We were thankful for each and every day.

Mike, George, Michael, Chris, Hank, and Eric

Chapter Eleven

#us·as·one

Chris had many challenges with his diagnosis, from short-term memory issues, expressive and receptive aphasia, vision challenges, headaches, changes in personality and mood, fatigue, nausea, seizures, and wounds. Sometimes, he lacked emotion with receptive aphasia. One morning, I came out to the family room visibly sad and said to Chris, "I cried in the shower today."
He responded, "I know you're talking to me, but I have no idea what you're saying."

Honestly, you would have thought I asked him for a soda. He had no idea what I was saying, nor could he understand my facial expressions. I quickly learned that there would be times of feeling broken-hearted because I knew he couldn't process or receive my emotions. We had lost so much over the seven years. I grieved for all we had lost and yet, at the same time was so thankful for all we still had. The duality of holding joy and grief at the same time is difficult to understand.

Communication is vital in a marriage, and we had to be very patient with one another. We often thought we should go to a marriage counselor because we weren't on the same page. Then, we would laugh and say, "LOL, this is way above their pay grade!!" We needed a counselor to help specifically with brain trauma. Ultimately, we brought everything to the Lord in the deepest of prayers. Sometimes, I would think to myself. "Oh goodness, we have lost one more thing together." Then, I would remember that God joined the two of us together to become one. 'Us as one' would always be enough.

Due to Chris' impaired speech, we played a game called 'guess what I'm thinking' throughout our day. He had anomic aphasia, which made it difficult to recall words… especially nouns. Thus, word finding proved to be very difficult. To build a sentence, he would provide descriptions of the word to get a cue, and then he would find his word with slow or halted speech. For example, our family was deciding where to eat for dinner one night. Chris said, "I know where to go." We waited as he circled for the name of the restaurant. Finally, he said, "We've been there twice. We went to it in Georgia. The menu is long. They have tons of desserts." When I finally guessed what he was talking about we were both relieved.

I loved to watch him work 'those circles' of thinking. This was the way we communicated, and we just encouraged others around us to join in for the game.

His conversation was vague. Sometimes, he would struggle to find the noun he wanted, so he would take the easy button and input the word "thing" in place of the noun. It's funny that I knew what he wanted, when "thing" was strung together in a sentence five times over. Likewise, we were uniquely challenged because he frequently changed his mind, like the color changes on a mood ring. For example, for two years I had wanted to get a dog. I knew I needed a pet to help me emotionally, and I also thought it would benefit Chris. His answer was always an emphatic "No!" He gave me several reasons why it wasn't a good idea. Then, one day out of nowhere, he said, "Go get the dog." I was shocked! Of course, I didn't know if I should believe him. So, I asked him multiple times each day for several weeks if we should get a dog. I also posed the question to him in a different cadence with some made-up sign language to see if he was processing well enough. For significant decisions, this was my strategy for communicating with him. I had to find his plumb line and ensure he wouldn't sway or change his mind. It often took those full two weeks, but then I could rest assured that I knew his answer. This was our constant, and this was our life. A few days later we got the dog. Millie, a miniature labradoodle from our 'sweet honeymoon location' of Lititz, PA.

Chris and Millie

Chapter Twelve

W.O.W.

Often, conversations would be difficult for Chris and a bit like 'Groundhog Day' for me. While we would enjoy our morning coffee, Chris would say, "I did my chores, took my pills, ate my fruit, and drank my three cups of water." So, I asked a dear friend, Ashley Ozmint, to professionally create chalkboard art with the fruits of the spirit. (Galatians 5:22-23) *"But the fruit of the Spirit is love, joy, peace, patience, kindness, goodness, faithfulness, gentleness, self-control; against such things, there is no law."* Because of this scripture, we could spark conversations and connect more. We talked about who we could show kindness to, how faithful God has been to us, and how we could demonstrate more patience to one another. This gave us topics of conversation even when we didn't have much action going on in our lives. I loved that we could share life on a deeper level. It was a great way to start our day! It was a great way to minister to others. Chris ministered to everyone he would see. He greeted every nurse, technician, and doctor with a smile and always wanted to hear more about their life. He loved others very well.

Chris enjoyed working in the yard every day. It was a place of productivity and time for prayer. It was also an opportunity for him to catch up with neighbors as they enjoyed their morning walk.

Before he started his day of yardwork, I would ask him to think of one thing he could share with me over our dinner time. Chris had the gift of wisdom, and I always wanted to hear his thoughts and heart. We started calling it his "Words of Wisdom" (W.O.W.) for the day. The words might have been few, but they were powerful and life-giving. I made a few videos of him sharing his W.O.W. about God's truths. I would then forward the videos to our family members, so that they could see him and enjoy life with him from a distance. They are true treasures in our hearts.

Chapter Thirteen

Purpose at the Gas Station

Chris would struggle to communicate when he was recovering from surgery, undergoing treatment, or dealing with the disease itself. Yet, despite his inability to communicate well, I would see glimpses of him. For example, he maintained his chivalry and still opened the car door for me out of his loving kindness. One morning, he took the fruit off his plate and put it on mine— a simple connection that meant a lot to me.

We always sought opportunities for him to do normal everyday activities. One of the things he loved to do was to go on errands with me and pump our gas. Honestly, I probably only pumped my gas ten times over two years. When my fuel tank started to run low, I would stop doing my errands, run by the house, and pick him up so he could get gas for me. This was really important for Chris because it made him feel needed. When he did this, he felt like he was doing something normal. He always wanted to have purpose and take care of me.

There was one gas station nearby that did not frustrate him because it was easy to operate. Therefore, we always went to this specific gas station. At that time, the screen on the gas pump did not ask the slew of questions such as: "Do you want a car wash?" "Are you a rewards member?" "What is your zip code?" Chris could not play the twenty-question game or even begin to read the promptings. The only question this pump needed was our PIN. So, I would roll down the window and tell him the PIN number one digit at a time. Chris would copy me after each number and trace it in the air with his finger until he understood it. Voila, he could pump gas! Each day was different, but he served and loved fully.

Chapter Fourteen

Love In Action

One afternoon, as we drove home from the dentist office, we passed an upscale restaurant. As we drove by, Chris said, "I really liked that restaurant. What is the name?" When I told him the name of the restaurant, he kept repeating it to himself over and over the entire ride home… Unbeknownst to me – he had huge plans!

He couldn't look things up on his phone, but he could speak into the phone to ask Google. He got the number for the restaurant and said to the manager, "I have brain cancer and want to have dinner with my wife for our anniversary. I want a table near the window, overlooking the city." So, on our anniversary night, he told me to wear a dress, and we were going somewhere special. When I asked what the restaurant was, he said he didn't remember the name, but trust me, I will find it. We drove through town and he pointed with his finger to turn either right or left. We landed at the restaurant, and I was completely amazed! We had our wonderful dinner and dessert, and our table overlooked the city of Columbia. The conversation was sparse, but I didn't care. We were together and he had planned the whole thing all by himself! Then he reached into his pocket and gave me a note. The note made me tear up. I loved every note he wrote in his final years. It would take a long time for him to get his thoughts into words and put them on paper. I could always figure it out even if the words weren't spelled correctly. They were the sweetest, warmest gifts and they were tender to my heart.

Chris and Sharon

NOTES

Weather we are in the coliseum on at home, being with you is all I will ever need. You ~~protomotot~~ pomplette me.

Chris

Chapter Fifteen

Folly Beach

Chris was on a low dose of steroid to reduce the swelling and headaches caused by the tumor. Over a long period of time, steroids have unwanted side effects, such as skin thinning. Nevertheless, we would keep him on a low dose of steroids to prevent seizures. Being on steroids was a give-and-take. For the last year-and-a-half of his life, I had to provide daily wound care for his wounds caused by steroids. To this day, I don't know how I managed it so well because I can't even look at the pictures I would send to his doctors. His skin was paper thin. I would often say to Chris, "Honey, I honestly want to put you in bubble wrap so you can't get hurt."

With 24/7 treatment, alarms, and sometimes four appointments a week – we yearned for a family vacation. One week while we were in Charleston for our clinic at MUSC, we decided to rent a VRBO on Folly Beach instead of staying at our typical med-stay hotel. The VRBO was large enough for our entire family and offered a beautiful marsh view. This is just what we needed. Chris could have quality time with the family and enjoy the beautiful scenery and sunsets overlooking the marsh. The kids and grandkids could choose to do as much, or as little, as they wanted. They could go to the beach, dine out, or explore, and then come back to share time with Chris. We were just twenty minutes from MUSC Research Hospital, which provided me with comfort if Chris were to have a seizure. After leaving the vacation house, I knew in my heart that our family needed this vacation. We needed a peaceful place for Chris to enjoy, for me to get respite, and for the kids to have fun!

When we were leaving the beach house I cried. Chris asked, "Why are you crying?" I told him that everyone facing the hardships of brain cancer should be able to enjoy a week of vacation at the beach while having the comfort of having MUSC nearby if they needed emergency medical assistance. I proceeded to tell him I wanted a house on Folly Beach with a marsh view and a ramp on the back for wheelchair accessibility. It was my dream to have a house like this available for glioblastoma patients and their families to enjoy. He responded laughingly, "Well, that would be a miracle." I said, with a Brazilian Carioca accent, "Fine, I will call it Cabana Miracle!" It is definitely a 'God-sized dream'. And now, the name for this dream vacation house for glioblastoma patients will be, "Palmetto Respite!" We will see if this dream comes true, so stay tuned....

Becca, Tatum Grace, Ryan, Hampton, Chris, Sharon, Mary Scott and Daniel
(An earlier beach visit)

Becca, Tatum Grace, Sharon, and Mary Scott
(An earlier beach visit)

*Chis and Sharon
Hampton and Tatum Grace
(An earlier beach visit)*

Chapter Sixteen

God Moments

In October 2021, Chris's tumor showed progression, so he got approved for Gamma Knife Surgery. They were able to target one tumor, but it was not safe to target the other tumor. In November, he fell and was injured. He was unable to understand me and struggled to control his mood. I was sure he would come out of it after three weeks when the swelling had reduced. Yet, it seemed like everybody around me noticed he wasn't doing well. Meanwhile, I'm just over here with my pom-poms saying to myself, "It's okay…we will get through this … again." Christmas 2021 came and went, but he didn't really know it was Christmas. Then, on January 5th, 2022, I noticed it had been five days without him going outside to blow off the driveway or walk the dog.

The following week, he had seizures back-to-back multiple days in a row. He was injured from his falls, which sadly kept happening while in the shower. Our youngest son, Daniel, and his wife were going to have their baby reveal party that upcoming Saturday. I called them daily and said, "Chris isn't doing well. Please tell your family I don't think we can join the party."

That Friday night, I told Chris, "Let's get you shaved, and I will pick out your clothes, and we can decide tomorrow morning if we can go to the party." Well, Saturday morning came. I was up early – showered, dressed, and eager to get Chris ready. He said he had a headache. But since he had a headache every single day, I pressed on. I got him dressed, grabbed his breakfast and medications, and told him he could get some good sleep on the drive up to Charlotte. Basically, I convinced him and myself that we could somehow make this trip. We got to the party and my daughter-in-law's uncle recognized Chris's need for assistance. He got Chris's food and tended to him throughout the evening. We enjoyed the wonderful reveal party. When we left, I hugged our family so tight and said, "This celebration was BETTER than Thanksgiving and Christmas, all wrapped up into one!" Tears were in my eyes. Somehow, I must have known deep in my heart what was about to come. We were so thankful we made it to the gathering of our grandbaby's party, and our hearts were full.

Chris, Daniel, and Mary Scott

Uncle Charles & Chris

This top picture was snapped as the cake revealed the color PINK. The new grandbaby would be a little girl! We soon came to find out her name was Elizabeth, named after Mary Scott's mom, who had passed away. And they would call her Eliza. Chris was so happy to know her name so that he could pray for her by name. And he said he already 'knew' Eliza because he saw the ultrasound photo. Daniel asked Chris to think of anything he wanted to share with Eliza one day. So, I would ask Chris at different times throughout the day when he was able to mentally process things clearly. I asked him what he would like to say to baby Eliza. Over time, I put together these few words – "Eliza is precious, and precious to the Lord." Wow, holding these words together is so beautiful! Our keepsake.

We were only at the party for an hour and then we drove back home. All Chris could say was, "Long, long." When we got home, he was talking gibberish. I fed him, gave him meds, and put him to bed. At 9 PM, I heard the shower turn on, and I was like, "No, not the shower!" I couldn't redirect him this time, so I showered him, and then he seized. I looked at him and said, "Chris, I know you aren't well, but I am here and will take care of you."

I tried to help him through the seizure and its after-effects and then had to take him to the emergency room. The neurologist came into Chris's room at 3 AM to talk with me. She gently held my hand and said, *"His neurology team doesn't have anything for him, and we don't have anything we can do for him. It's time to take him home."* I understood. I called hospice the following day.

Chapter Seventeen

Thank You

Chris had told me two times in early January that he didn't think it would be long until he passed away. I said, "Chris, November is when you started falling, and things were getting more difficult for you." *I was encouraged to know that this was never my battle to fight. It was almost as if God were saying to me, "Release Chris to me and rest in me."* Thus, I chose the word '*REST*' for my 2022 focus word.

From November to February, his decline was fast and arduous. The last seven nights were just awful. He was up all night, uncomfortable, unsettled, and not well. In hindsight, I wish I would have had a plan in place to have one of Chris's siblings or a caregiver team to stay with me 24/7 through Hospice, because he was completely dependent on me. I know it was God's strength that I managed through each day and the exhausting nights. In the mornings, my sister-in-law Ellen came to the house to clean everything. She helped me do laundry and tended to Chris so I could close my eyes for a moment. Chris wanted to pass at the house, and I wanted that for him. On night number eight, I put him to bed, and within forty-five minutes, I knew we were off to a tough night. My sister-in-law Judy came over, and we teamed up to help Chris. Even with both of us tending to him, it was not enough. We didn't have enough meds prescribed to help him pass away comfortably at home. I called the hospice house the following morning to see if they had an open room for him. Thankfully, they did. It was a long morning to wait from 7:30 AM until the transport arrived at 11 AM. I sat on the side of the bed holding Chris's right side, embracing his arm and rocking him gently. I said, "Chris, I'm right here beside you, and I'll never leave you. I Love You, and God is going to take care of you and God is going to take care of me." He slowly tracked to the right with distant eyes and whispered softly, *"Thank You."*

This world has lost a wonderful human and faithful servant to our Lord. He was a true fighter who kept the most peaceful and accepting attitude throughout his journey. Heaven is rejoicing to have such a beautiful angel.

It was the last word he spoke to me, and I will hold onto this treasure for eternity. I am blessed with such deep gratitude for my husband and for my Lord.

Sharon Mercer

Chris was admitted to Agape Hospice House at 11 AM on Thursday and passed away at 5 PM on Friday evening with his sons and me at his side. He was under hospice care for three short weeks.

Faith Is Everything

"I have fought the good fight, I have finished the race, I have kept the faith."

2 Timothy 4:7 (NIV)

Chapter Eighteen

Full Circle

Chris worked for an IT service company called Computer Sciences Corporation (CSC) for 29 years. CSC was a multinational software corporation that frequently transferred employees from the India offices to work locally in Columbia, SC. He was a director/project manager and led a team of Indian employees. Whenever he had a new Indian employee come stateside, he wanted to welcome them warmly. So, he often invited them to join our family for dinner or include them in a family event. Chris wanted to be available to them and help them in any way.

One Sunday after church, we went out for lunch. While we were eating, Chris said, "I didn't hear a thing the pastor said today." And I responded, "Oh my gosh, that's happened to me before too." And he said, "No… I couldn't even listen to the message because God was putting this verse on my heart." He shared *Ephesians 2:10 (NIV), "For we are*

God's handiwork, created in Christ Jesus to do good works, which God prepared in advance for us to do."

He said, "Sharon, I think God's telling us we need to move to Windsor Shore apartments. I believe if we don't go, we will be disobedient." I responded, "WOW! God is taking me full circle!" {*Our family was stationed in Wellington, India. I was four years old, and my father attended the Defense Service Staff College for the Armed Forces training institution.*}

So, we farmed out our two dogs, which were too large to live in the apartment, and we moved our family to Windsor Shores. It was only a short distance from our house – three miles. After we got settled in, we had a party at the Windsor Shores Clubhouse. We invited all the Indian staff and their families to join us, and we catered Indian Cuisine. It was wonderful to meet everyone Chris had spoken so highly of and to be introduced to their spouses and children.

Chris gathered everyone together and asked for the blessing over our dinner. And then he said, "Is anyone curious why I moved my family to Windsor Shores?" A few people piped up, and one raised his hand and said, "Because you are our manager, and you want to keep an eye on us."

And Chris said, "Well, I'm your manager – but that's not why we relocated. I don't want to be known as just your manager… I want to be known as your friend. And I feel like the only way we could have a true friendship was to live where you live."

So basically, our Indian friends became our extended family, and we became like an aunt and uncle as they were mostly in their young 20s and 30s. We had many Indian potluck dinners, taught swimming lessons, had afternoon walks, late evening visits over chai tea, played cricket on the tennis courts, and had baby showers at the Clubhouse. Everyone's apartment was like a revolving door – we just did life together!

Riddhi Medidi 💗
Christmas Eve Candlelight service

Chris, Sharon, DJ, Sunil, and Manasi

Chris and Anirudh Bagchi

Chris with Anirudh Bagchi

They left their lovely house and moved into a 2-bedroom apartment. That's where we started the friendships with not only our family, but all the other 40-50 Indian families living there.

- Rohini Bagchi
CSC Employee From India

Spoken Words From Family

Ryan Mercer

When my dad was diagnosed with brain cancer in 2015, it came as quite a shock. I was in medical school at the time, so I felt like I had more insight than most people when it came to the journey that lay ahead. I remember my brother and others coming up to me and asking, "What does this mean?" or "Is there a cure?"

My heart broke because I knew there wasn't a cure. I knew the prognosis was bleak. I knew he probably only had about 12 months to live.

Questions went through my mind as well: "Will my dad see me get married?" "Will my dad see my brother get married?" "Will my dad ever meet his grandchildren?" I was concerned for his future, my brother's future, my mother's future, and my future all at once.

That amount of worry can be paralyzing. What was even more difficult was seeing someone who was so brilliant lose his ability to process things. It was difficult seeing menial tasks become so difficult for him.

For example, my mom would ask, "Chris, can you run inside and get me some milk from the grocery store." He would come back out 10 minutes later with coffee creamer. Things like this began to pile up year after year until he couldn't quite take care of himself anymore. He would need to be reminded of things like taking a bath and brushing his teeth, and eventually, he would need help performing these tasks.

Seven years later, and many stories later, we gathered together to celebrate my dad's life at his funeral. It was a whirlwind of memories and too much to put into one book. If there were something I would like to leave the reader with, it is this...

I think it is easy to focus on all the difficulties and negatives when it comes to cancer. To be honest, cancer is difficult, and it is very hard to see a loved one experience it. However, I hope that this book will bring to light some of the positives in the midst of a difficult diagnosis. This book won't cure the disease, but I hope it comforts your heart and lets you know that you are not alone.

Paige and Mark Fisher (In-Laws)

Ryan, Chris, and Daniel

Chris and Ryan

Becca, Ryan, Carol, Sharon, Chris, Tatum Grace, and Hampton

Chris and Ryan

Chris and Hampton

Spoken Words From Family

Mary Scott Mercer

Mary Scott and Eliza
(Daniel and Mary Scott's Daughter)

My name is Mary Scott Mercer, and I am married to Daniel Mercer. Daniel is Sharon and Chris's younger son. We started dating about ten years ago. So, I knew Chris before he was diagnosed with brain cancer. We got engaged after his diagnosis in our junior year of college. We were married the following year in May. There was a point where things got pretty serious. We thought about hurrying our wedding date so he would be a part of it. But as we all know, he lived much longer than we thought.

That January, we went on a family cruise. After the family cruise, Chris started demonstrating some abnormal signs. He tripped, going up the stairs. Things would happen, and he would not remember. He had a tumor growing in his brain, but we did not know it at the time. That journey was very interesting. Ironically, my mom passed away when I was sixteen, so my story includes parental loss and illness. Walking through that with the Mercers was interesting because I could share my experience and relate to chronic and life-threatening illnesses in many ways. So I think it was really cool and good timing to be a supportive member of their family, even though we weren't married yet. Daniel's response was very emotional when we found out Chris had brain cancer. Chris was very connected with both of his sons.

The journey was seven years long, similar to my experience of losing my mom. It was one of those things where people gradually grieved him with time, which is harder in many ways. Still, it's better because you can make peace along the way versus having an overnight tragedy that some people experience with losing a parent or a loved one. I witnessed each family member grieve parts of him over time, specifically Sharon; she was probably the most upset. She was severely shocked in the early parts when she lost the main versions of him as her husband. She created a new relationship with him that was very patient and caregiver-centered, but she did what she could to honor those parts of him that she still could. That gave him dignity and manhood in many ways, which I think many people in her shoes would have a tough time doing. She treated him with humanness and dignity. She treated him like an adult, even though he often seemed very childlike.

There were different phases of his brain cancer. Huge parts of him changed. Maybe he went through a spell where he was angry, or he couldn't read or speak as much, but then he would also have these childlike episodes, which were funny at times. They would go out to eat, and she would have to order for him. Or he might throw a temper tantrum; it was ironic and funny simultaneously because you learn to laugh about how much things have changed. I think Chris had some amazing abilities at times to be his old self when his boys struggled with something in life and needed him, even when I needed him to be a father to me in many ways. He would step into that mode in really bizarre ways. One day, he may not be able to think as clearly, but the next day, when you need him to parent and guide you, he'd be able to, which was special.

One thing Sharon did that was lifesaving for her was her binge toward positivity and seeing the good parts of the situation. She tried as hard as possible to keep life light and fun despite the tragedy in many ways. It was her way of surviving. She created fun memories, took photos, and went out to eat as much as possible. It is essential to make things positive or to keep life functional for you as the caregiver. That's how she did it.

Over time, one thing I noticed, specifically watching Sharon as a caregiver, was the loneliness that came with losing the emotional part of her marriage and her need to find connection and depth. The emotional touch with us as the other family members because she lost that ability with Chris over time. She very much stepped into the role of caring for him. His ability to attune to her needs or emotions became less and less. Finding community and people you feel safe to be real with are vital. She really had to lean on us for those things.

We spent a ton of time with Sharon and Chris. Ryan and Becca lived in Columbia, Missouri, and Myrtle Beach for a large chunk of the seven-year diagnosis. Daniel and I were with them constantly. In many ways, we were caregivers for both of them. Sharon would have pretty significant flares with Rheumatoid Arthritis. That would impact her ability to care for him, depending on whether she could walk. It was adorable because Chris was mentally disabled with his brain tumor, but he was physically himself, which was amazing. They made one complete person because she would help him mentally and emotionally. We were their primary people for most of those years.

I went on every family vacation. Chris would have episodes at times where his skin would be very thin based on medication. During one vacation, he had a lot of open wounds and cuts. We were in Folly Beach in the summer, which is very hot. He would have to walk around in pants and sweatshirts to ensure he didn't accidentally bump the wall too hard and have a bruise that would bleed or cut himself. We would go with him to Walmart. In the summertime at the beach, finding long pants and long-sleeved shirts is challenging because they were never available. It was always fun and exciting to explain that he sometimes couldn't get what he wanted. He could communicate wants and desires but making some happen would be like jumping through hurdles. Still, Sharon would go above and beyond to make him happy and allow him to live his life the best he could, whether going to Lowe's a million times a week or getting a new yard tool. He loved doing yard work. He could still contribute. He spent many days there. His yard was absolutely beautiful and immaculate. He walked around all day, picking up every pinecone, every leaf, and every gumball that fell. He would be like a version of his old self, which was really sweet.

He showed a love for me as if I were his daughter. Even though I married into their family, he treated me like a daughter he had never had, which was special. He would always snap back and offer kind advice or pray for me if we needed something, which was really tender and memorable. This relationship and circumstance really bonded my relationship with Sharon in many ways. From losing my mom, it's been sweet and redemptive to have a close relationship with my mother-in-law and walk this road with her all these years.

He would try to find sweet ways of loving Sharon. He would write love notes with scribble because his penmanship and ability to write and read suffered. He would always find ways to write little love letters or get her gifts. He would call Daniel and me to help him buy her Christmas gifts. He still really tried to show his love for her and thank her for how she cared for him. Despite everything that was happening mentally with Chris, there was a ten-second pause where he came to and was able to thank her for all she had done for him. In many ways, she laid down her life for him at a significant cost of her physical well-being because of the stress of all these years taking care of someone who needed her. It had a tremendous physical impact on her, and he thanked her right before he passed, which was really tender.

Chris and Mary Scott

Sharon, Chris, Daniel,
Mary Scott, Mark, and Shelley

Chris, Shelley, Sharon, and Mark

Chris and Daniel

Hampton, Daniel, Chris, and Ryan

Ryan, Chris, Sharon, Daniel, and Mary Scott

Chris, Daniel, Mary Scott, Ryan, Hampton,
Becca, Sharon, and Carol

Spoken Words From Family

Marilyn Nicolaisen

Sharon and I are cousins. So, I've known her my whole life. Our families would visit each other as often as geography allowed since Sharon's family was in the military. My sister, Dacia, Sharon, and I were considered the Three Musketeers, but the girl version. We loved being together, even though there was a little age difference. Sharon and I formed a lasting bond when I lived with her and her family in Brazil. We became Christians at the same time and were baptized together. I didn't meet Sharon's husband, Chris, for quite a while because we lived far apart. We had our children, and our lives became very busy. Sharon's parents built a beautiful home in the Georgia Mountains called Camp JillyBob. I would bring my two daughters, niece, and nephew, and we would meet Sharon and her sons at Camp JillyBob and have a week or two of fun. Sharon always called it cousin camp since we were cousins, and our kids were second cousins. We enjoyed spending time together and praying for each other.

As the years passed, we both became empty nesters. Chris was transferred to Pennsylvania, and we went to Lancaster and spent a weekend with them. Then, at the beginning of 2015, Chris had a health scare. She called me a lot because they were trying to figure out what was wrong with Chris, and then sadly, he received his brain cancer diagnosis. Around the same time, Sharon's mother was having issues with Parkinson's, so I went to Georgia to help her mother with doctor's appointments since Sharon needed to be with Chris. Sharon's mother wanted to see her because she hadn't seen her since Chris was diagnosed. So, my aunt and I drove to Sharon's in South Carolina since they had moved back. Since that time, Sharon and I have become even closer. I felt that the Lord put on my heart that everybody would be focused on Chris – and Sharon, his caretaker, could easily be overlooked. I knew my focus was supposed to be on Sharon and ensuring she had what she needed physically, spiritually, emotionally, and mentally. That's the mantle I felt the Lord put on me. She was Chris's advocate, and I needed to be hers. We would talk on the phone and FaceTime a lot. One important way Sharon says that I had lasting impact and which was a lifesaver for her was when I showed her the iPhone Notes app. She could put all her questions and concerns for the doctor, all the answers, Chris' medicines, and pretty much anything she needed to "note" so she could stay organized and on top of things. Numerous people cared for Chris and Sharon; people were constantly at their house. It was open 24 hours.

Caring for Chris and all of the people there to visit and "help" was taking a huge toll on Sharon, as evidence in her worsening RA symptoms. I told her that she needed to set some boundaries. So, she would put out a sign when Chris was sleeping – so she herself could take a moments rest. A lifesaving idea I gave Sharon was that she needed to create a sanctuary for herself in the house – a place to recharge, rest, and do whatever was needed. Another way I cared for Sharon was to visit periodically to provide an "escape" and help with Chris. She and I would have some fun and normality. Just being with Sharon also encourages me because she loves so deeply.

I am blessed to have been able to walk with Sharon through this difficult experience. I tried to be available when she wanted to FaceTime, call, or just needed to vent to tell me about the latest health scare or crazy thing Chris did. And sometimes, she just needed to laugh or cry. Sharon embodies how to walk through something difficult with faith, love, grace, and, above all, the joy of the Lord, as evidenced in this book. Her love and giving heart truly inspire me.

Cousins: Marilyn, Sharon, and Dacia

Chris and Marilyn

STEPL

Music is a miraculous gift! STEPL has been together since 1997. They present a varied program of Christian music, including contemporary praise and worship, Southern, Traditional, and a bit of urban gospel. The group comprises David Spears, Kent Beasley, Jud Kinsey, and John Husband. They have performed at churches, community, and civic functions throughout South Carolina, parts of Georgia, North Carolina, Alabama, and Vermont.

December 22, before Chris passed in February, our dearest friends, the Fishers (now our in-laws), asked STEPL to have a private caroling at their house on Christmas Eve. It was just the Fisher family, our son Ryan, his wife Becca, and kids Chris, me, and STEPL. It was a beautiful private concert and a gift to us all. They sang five songs, and the last song STEPL sang was "I Can See the Light!" Chris had his arms raised above his head, his eyes closed, praising the Lord in the truest form. He was so joyful! This is a moment I will never forget.

David Spears, Kent Beasley,
Chris, Jud Kinsey, John Husband

Brain Tumor Awareness Month Brochure

"Rejoicing in hope, patient in tribulation, continuing steadfastly in prayer." Romans 12:12

The Brain Cancer Caregiver Companion
Our Story

Meeting the Challenges
of Brain Cancer as a Devoted Caregiver:

Travel has been part of Sharon Mercer's life since childhood. She grew up as a military brat and lived in several bases in the United States and abroad, including Kuwait, Egypt, India, and Brazil. She worked for American Express International Travel and then independent travel until her husband, Chris, was diagnosed with anaplastic astrocytoma.

"It was all happening so fast. Our world shifted, and we were now learning how to navigate life with brain cancer," recalls Sharon.

It was four years ago that Chris suffered two seizures that left him unable to speak. At first, the couple thought they were transient ischemic attacks or mini-strokes. Chris learned of his brain tumor after his third episode. He had several treatments, including brain surgery, while he was awake. He also enrolled in a clinical trial for an experimental treatment but was later removed from the study due to the progression of the tumor. Chris' brain tumor and treatments have affected his personality, mood, short-term memory, eyesight, and especially communication with his loved ones. Chris is currently taking three medications to manage the effects of his brain tumor.

"There are so many ups and downs in this journey for Chris, yet I try to stay flexible and adjust to his needs." Sharon viewed Chris's health as a priority. She felt it was necessary to put herself second as a caregiver. "When Chris was first diagnosed with a brain tumor, I was really struggling emotionally, physically, and mentally, and because I couldn't lean on my husband for help, I knew I needed to find support."

Helpful Notes from a
Brain Cancer Caregiver

- **Create a small support team:**
  - ➤ Family support
  - ➤ Brain Tumor Counselor Support from Oncologists
  - ➤ A Point-of-Contact to help relay info or make calls
  - ➤ Ones that can help with errands and organizing food
  - ➤ Ones that you can be vulnerable with and lean on in hard moments
  - ➤ Ones that will get things done— "The Worker Bees"
  - ➤ Deciphering what only you can do and delegating other daily tasks to others, (house cleaners, yard work, etc.)

- **Set up an account with <u>CaringBridge.org</u>** to keep friends and family up to date in one place.

- **KEEP a list of <u>Pathology Report Information</u>** to note the biomarkers and genetic mutations. Maintain record keeping for all the surgeries, treatment dates, and changes.

- **Prior to clinic**, take notes of any questions, thoughts, concerns, and journal updates - to ensure they will be covered during the office visit with the neuro-oncologist.

- **Location:** In addition to understanding the brain cancer diagnosis and treatment -- <u>tumor location</u> is important because many of the brain tumor symptoms are related to the tumor lobe area. Knowing the location of the tumor will allow you understanding of the symptoms and actions your loved one is experiencing.

- **Neurocognitive and Neurobehavioral effects:** The following are some of the most common Brain Cancer Symptoms: headaches, seizures, changes in personality or irritability, vision problems, memory loss, attention deficits, mood swings, tingling, or stiffness on one side of the body, behavioral changes, loss of balance, nausea, fatigue, language difficulties/aphasia, muscle weakness, loss of coordination, feeling confused or disoriented, and impaired reasoning and processing.

- **Cognitive and Neurological changes, along with treatments create daily challenges.** The day in the life of a brain cancer caregiver is ever-changing -- from personal care, mobility, decision making, communicating, transportation, housework, meal preparation, coordinating medical care, managing therapy and medications, managing side effects, managing finances, managing wounds, and the list goes on.

- **Tools to cultivate as a caregiver.**
  - ➢ Peace
  - ➢ Patience
  - ➢ Care
  - ➢ Love
  - ➢ Encouragement
  - ➢ Flexibility

Are just some of the tools that help support and advocate for your loved ones.

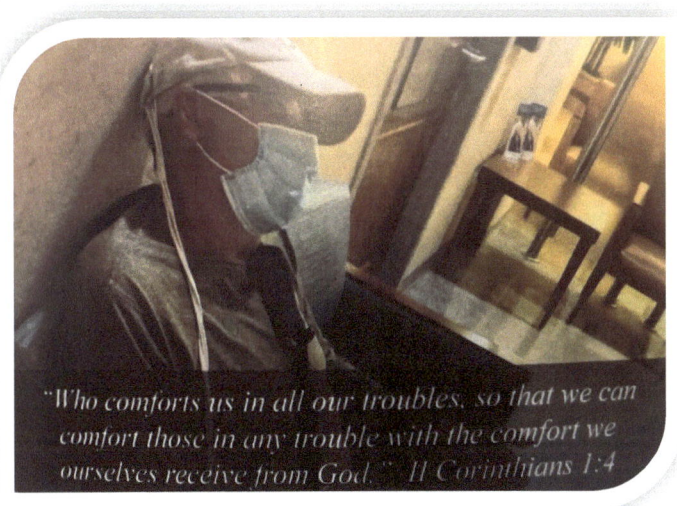

"Who comforts us in all our troubles, so that we can comfort those in any trouble with the comfort we ourselves receive from God." II Corinthians 1:4

COVID19 Times

- Because visitors are limited or not allowed into hospitals, have a NOTES page to be "ER-ready" with patients' information:

  - ➢ Name
  - ➢ DOB
  - ➢ Neuro Oncologists
  - ➢ Treatment facility
  - ➢ Diagnosis
  - ➢ Craniotomy dates
  - ➢ Treatment changes
  - ➢ Current medications
  - ➢ How seizures present & what meds to stabilize
  - ➢ Your contact number

"I lift my eyes to the mountains – where does my help come from? My help comes from the Lord the maker of Heaven and Earth."
Psalm 121:1-2

Take Care of YOU!!

- **Being a caregiver is a marathon!** If the caregiver is not in a healthy place, no one is. The emotional impact of the diagnosis and treatment can be daunting. So here are a few ideas to help you move forward each day and plan for a necessary respite!

Proper rest/sleep
Good nutrition
Drink H2O
daily prayer
warm bath
Set goals
Family/friends
Breathe slowly
count your blessings
Walk and exercise daily
Nature/Park/Picnic/Swing
Golf/Swim/bike/gym
Sunshine & fresh air
Puzzle/game/Read
fresh flowers in home

Quiet time each day
Live in THE moment
Time off
take a day trip
gardening
Massage
Play piano
Unplug from technology
Serve others
Movie/fun
Listen to favorite music
Counseling from SW
Seek brain tumor support
Make a gratitude list
Ask for help!

**Take action! What brings you?
Joy / Peace / Relaxation.**

Sharon reached out to the ABTA to find that support and was able to receive guidance on financial resource options, insurance and brain tumor treatments. She was connected to a nurse to help understand MRI reports and learned strategies to help her cope with caregiving for her husband. Now, she asks for help from family and friends to assist Chris, like taking him to an appointment or driving him to places.

It has been four years since the initial diagnosis, and Sharon continues to work toward finding a healthy balance when caring for her husband and herself. When things are really overwhelming, she takes time to rest and refresh, such as staying at a nearby bed and breakfast. The time away not only helps Sharon, but she also comes back recharged and ready to care for her husband again.

The most important thing Sharon did for herself, with the help of the ABTA, was to partner with a mentor who also walked along a similar journey.

"This was the biggest blessing. My mentor, Robin, embraced me," said Sharon. "She heard and got my story. She was there for me when the diagnosis of brain cancer was so devastating."

The ability to connect with someone who understands the brain tumor experience, like a peer mentor, can be comforting and healing. It doesn't take away the diagnosis and all the fears that come with it, but it lets people know that they are not alone, according to Vince Rock, MSW, ABTA program manager, who leads the ABTA

CommYOUnity Connect mentorship program. The program has made over 600 mentor-mentee matches since May 2015.

"This connection between a peer mentor and mentee can be powerful. Several of our mentors have told us they never had a mentor of their own, and they want to offer that support to someone who is walking in the same shoes," says Vince.

Robin is still Sharon's mentor to this day, and they've had the opportunity to meet each other and their respective families on their travels.

*H*O*P*E*
Carry HOPE Daily!

I have found several
Brain Cancer Resources
that provide Council/ support/
guidance services:

- ABTA.org for a "mentor" to walk you through this journey as a brain cancer caregiver. In addition, ABTA provides resources to support the complex needs of the brain cancer patient and caregiver.

- Brain Tumor Network: to speak with a Nurse Liaison or Brain Cancer Social Worker for support. They will also help with navigating Government Clinical Trials.

Additional Brain Cancer Foundations can assist with support, resources, money, medical treatments, transportation to/from clinics, bills, etc.

- ❖ Musella Foundation **download**

- ❖ <u>Brain Tumor Guide For The Newly Diagnosed</u>

- ❖ Michael Matters

- ❖ The Sontag Foundation

- ❖ Glenn Garcelon Foundation

- ❖ Missions 4 Maureen

- ❖ Darren Dalton Foundation

Notes from a Brain Cancer Caregiver

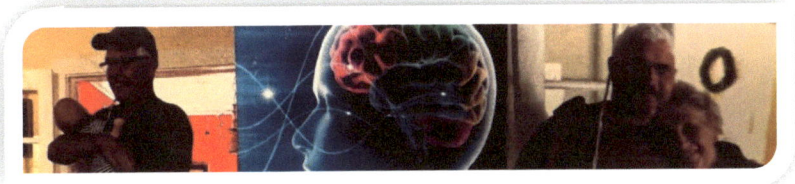

Although there are many
challenges with
brain cancer, every day
is a blessing!

Find the "new normal" and
help your loved one maintain
independence and enjoy life.

There will be limitations,
but help your loved one
do all they can!

Celebrate
each day as a gift,
one day at a time!

www.ingramcontent.com/pod-product-compliance
Lightning Source LLC
Chambersburg PA
CBHW040851120626
46547CB00006B/565